ELECTION CAMPAIGNS

A Kid's Guide

by Emma Carlson Berne

CAPSTONE PRESS
a capstone imprint

Captivate is published by Capstone Press, an imprint of Capstone.
1710 Roe Crest Drive, North Mankato, Minnesota 56003
www.capstonepub.com

Library of Congress Cataloging-in-Publication Data
Library of Congress Cataloging-in-Publication data is available on the Library of Congress website.
ISBN 978-1-5435-9208-5 (library binding)
ISBN 978-1-4966-6606-2 (paperback)
ISBN 978-1-5435-9209-2 (eBook PDF)

Summary: Gives facts about election campaigns and how they are a part of U.S. elections.

Image Credits
Alamy: Jeffrey Isaac Greenberg 3, 23, Jim West, 15, Richard Ellis, 18, The Photo Works, 22, Tribune Content Agency LLC, 16; Getty Images: Photo 12/Contributor, 25; Newscom: CandidatePhotos/Chris Fitzgerald, 14, CQ Roll Call/Bill Clark, 20, CQ Roll Call/Tom Williams, 28, LA Opinion/Aurelia Ventura, 17, MCT/Joe Cavaretta, 8-9, Reuters/Brian Snyder, 21, Reuters/Carlo Allegri, 7, Sipa USA/Globe Photos, 6, TNS/Chris Seward, 24, ZUMA Press/Ronen Tivony, 29; Shutterstock: Andy Dean Photography, 27, David Gilder, 13, Joseph Sohm, 5, Matt Smith Photographer, 11, Michael F. Hiatt, 19, michelmond, 12, mikeledray, 4, Rob Crandall, 26, Tetiana Yurchenko, Cover, 1

Design Elements
Capstone; Shutterstock: openeyed, GarganTul

Editorial Credits
Editor: Michelle Parkin; Designer: Bobbie Nuytten;
Media Researcher: Jo Miller; Production Specialist: Laura Manthe

All internet sites appearing in back matter were available and accurate when this book was sent to press.

Printed in the United States of America.
PA99

Table of Contents

Glossary terms are **bold** on first use.

Part of Democracy

In the United States, we vote for our leaders in government. But how do leaders get elected? How do they let voters know who they are and what they stand for? People running for office use political campaigns. In a political campaign, a person tries to convince voters that he or she would do the best job in an elected position.

Donald Trump spoke at a campaign event in 2016.

Barack Obama during his election campaign in 2012

A person running for office is called a candidate. Candidates can run in three different types of elections—local elections, state elections, and national elections. Local elections are for candidates who want to work in the community. This includes judges, school board or city council members, and sheriffs. In state elections, candidates can run for governor, as well as positions in **Congress**. Candidates who want to become U.S. president or vice president run in national elections.

FACT: George Washington was America's first president. He was elected in 1789.

Ready, Set, Run!

Let's say a person wants to run for U.S. president. It's not enough to tell neighbors and friends. A candidate has to get his or her message out to voters. Candidates do this during the political campaign. Political campaigns take place before the election.

In 2019 Julián Castro announced he was running for president.

President Trump spoke during his campaign to be reelected president.

Starting the Campaign

To begin a campaign, the presidential candidate makes an announcement. An announcement is a speech that introduces the candidate to people around the country. Newspapers, TV stations, and social media pages may feature articles or interviews about the candidate after the announcement. Soon, a lot of people will know the person is running for president.

FACT: **Citizens** who are at least 18 years old can vote in U.S. elections.

During the **general election**, candidates from different **political parties** run against each other. But hang on! Before that happens, a candidate needs to win the **primary election**. Primary elections are like general elections, but they are between members of the same political party.

Let's say five candidates from the Democratic Party want to be president. They will run against each other in a primary election. Candidates in the Republican Party will do the same. Voters choose one winner from each party.

POLITICS IS A PARTY

Candidates are members of political parties. Political parties are groups of people who have similar values and positions on issues. The two main parties are the Democratic Party and the Republican Party. There are also smaller political parties, such as the Libertarian Party and the Green Party. Candidates can also be Independents.

Republican candidates ran against each other in 2008.

Let's Talk About Platforms

Your candidate won the primary election! But don't celebrate yet. Now he or she has to run against candidates from other parties. It's time to campaign for the general election. Candidates have a big job. They have to tell as many voters as possible about their political **platforms**. This isn't the type of platform you stand on. It's what you stand *for*. A political platform is what a candidate plans to do if elected.

FACT: Different ideas in a platform are called planks.

Let's say people in a community think there are too many potholes in their city roads. A candidate's platform could include how he or she plans to pay for road repairs. In a national election, presidential candidates could talk about taxes and gun control in their platforms.

Presidential candidate Hillary Clinton spoke to voters in Pennsylvania.

One way for a candidate to start the campaign is to hold a **rally**. At a rally, people who support the candidate come together in one place. The candidate makes a speech. He or she lays out a platform. Voters hear the candidate's solutions to the country's problems.

Presidential candidate Beto O'Rourke held a rally in Houston, Texas.

Candidate Rob Quist held a rally during his campaign for U.S. House of Representatives.

Candidates also try to raise money during these rallies. Candidates need a lot of money to keep their campaigns running. They need to fly to different places for rallies and speeches. Money is also used for TV ads, T-shirts, flyers, and other items to get people to vote.

To run a successful campaign, candidates ask people to **donate** money. Some people might give a few dollars. Others might give hundreds of dollars. But people can't give too much to campaigns. According to the law, a person can give a candidate up to $2,800 per election.

Donations were collected for Mike Huckabee during his presidential campaign.

The donation limit is meant to help keep campaigns fair. Imagine if a voter gave a candidate a huge amount of money during the campaign. Eventually, the candidate becomes president. The new president may feel the need to help the voter who gave all that money. That would be unfair to other people.

Supporters gave money to Bernie Sanders's campaign.

Campaign Staff and Support

Campaigns are a lot of work. Candidates can't do them alone. That's why they have help. Two types of people work on campaigns—staff and **volunteers**. Campaign staff are paid employees. Their jobs are to run parts of the campaign. One person might talk to reporters or set up interviews. Another might keep track of donations.

Staff members and volunteers worked at the Travis County Democratic Office in Texas.

Student volunteers answered phone calls during a campaign in California.

Campaigns also use a lot of volunteers. Volunteers are unpaid. They are regular people who want to help the candidate get elected. Campaign volunteers do a number of different jobs. They call voters and talk about the candidate's platform. They ask people to donate money. Volunteers might go door-to-door and tell voters about their candidate. Volunteers can also post online about rallies.

Meeting Voters

It's not enough for candidates to go to rallies and give speeches. A good candidate wants to hear from people. Many candidates hold town hall meetings. These meetings take place in community centers or auditoriums. Voters get to ask the candidate questions in front of the group. This is the time to talk about concerns and worries voters have.

Presidential candidate Marco Rubio answered questions at a town hall meeting.

Candidates also stop by places where voters are, including restaurants, libraries, coffee shops, and barber shops. They introduce themselves. They tell voters why they are running for office. They listen to what people have to say.

Senator Kamala Harris spoke to supporters in Des Moines, Iowa.

Candidates even knock on people's doors. This is called **canvassing**. Candidates make sure to wear name tags so people know who they are. A candidate may bring a clipboard to write down comments people make. The candidate could give a postcard with his or her picture on it. This will help people remember the candidate on Election Day.

Candidate Bryan Caforio canvassed a neighborhood in California.

Presidential candidate Cory Booker talked to staff and volunteers before canvassing in New Hampshire.

Meeting with the candidate in small groups and one-on-one gives people a chance to see who the candidate is. Some voters ask about the other people running for office. Voters want to know why the candidate disagrees with others in the race.

Talk It Out

A candidate can't meet with every single voter. Campaign ads help. Candidates can pay for ads on TV and the radio. They also have social media accounts. Posting regularly helps candidates interact with voters online. The other candidates will have ads and online posts too.

An "I Voted" social media page

A campaign commercial for President Barack Obama in 2012

Sometimes, candidates talk negatively about each other. Negative TV ads often appear in black and white with scary music in the background. These ads prey on people's fears and emotions. It's important for voters to research each candidate and his or her platform. They shouldn't believe everything they see about candidates on TV.

At some point, all of the candidates will face each other and hold a **debate**. This often happens in presidential elections.

During a debate, the candidates meet in a large room, such as an auditorium or a theater. They stand in front of an audience. A **moderator** asks a question. Each candidate gets a chance to answer. This is a candidate's chance to talk about his or her platform. It's a serious discussion with other people running for the same position.

Candidates for governor of North Carolina debated in 2016.

FACT: Political debates have been around a long time. In 1858, Abraham Lincoln and Stephen Douglas debated seven times on campaign stops.

FACT: The first presidential debate on TV was between John F. Kennedy and Richard Nixon in 1960. Kennedy won the election and became president in 1961.

John F. Kennedy

Richard Nixon

The time has come. It's Election Day! That means the campaign is over. The candidates have done all they can to earn votes. Presidential elections are held every four years. They are always on the day after the first Monday in November.

People voted for president on Election Day in 2008.

News coverage of President Trump giving his acceptance speech in 2016

Candidates usually watch the election results with family and supporters. When the votes have been counted, the winner makes an acceptance speech. The loser makes a speech too. Even if they lose, it's important for candidates to thank their supporters.

You and Political Campaigns

You can't vote in an election yet. But don't worry. You can get involved in political campaigns right now. Campaigns welcome kid volunteers. Ask a parent or older sibling to drive you to the office of your favorite candidate. You may be able to prepare mailings, do office tasks, or answer the phone. Go with an adult door-to-door and talk about your candidate.

Candidate Jason Lewis met with student volunteers at his campaign office.

Senator Cory Booker with students from Cheyenne High School

You may be able to organize a mock election in school. Talk to your teacher about how to get involved. On Election Day, wear a T-shirt with your favorite candidate's name on it. Ask a parent to take you with when voting. You can see what voting is like up close. Find out what you can about campaigns now. Who knows? Maybe you'll be running your own political campaign some day!

Glossary

canvass (KAN-vuhss)—to ask people for opinions or votes

citizen (SI-tuh-zuhn)—a member of a country or state who has the right to live there

Congress (KAHN-gruhs)—the part of the U.S. government that makes laws; Congress is made up of the Senate and the House of Representatives

debate (di-BAYT)—discussion with sides with different views

donate (DOH-nate)—to give something as a gift

general election (JEN-ur-uhl i-LEK-shuhn)—an election that is held in all the states at the same time

moderator (MOD-uhr-rayt-ohr)—a person who directs and leads a meeting

platform (PLAT-fohrm)—a statement of beliefs

political party (puh-LIT-uh-kuhl PAR-tee)—a group of people who share the same views about how government should run

primary election (PRYE-mair-ee i-LEK-shuhn)—an election in which voters choose the party candidates who will run for office

rally (RAL-ee)—a large gathering of people with similar interests

volunteer (vol-uhn-TIHR)—a person who chooses to do work without pay

Read More

Cunningham, Kevin. *How Political Campaigns and Elections Work.* Minneapolis: Core Library, 2015.

Gunderson, Jessica. *Understanding Your Role in Elections.* North Mankato, MN: Capstone Press, 2018.

Wil, Mara. *Electing Leaders.* Ann Arbor, MI: Cherry Lake Publishing, 2017.

Internet Sites

Kids Voting USA
https://kidsvotingusa.org/

Win the White House
https://www.icivics.org/games/win-white-house

Index